Johnson's®

Your Baby
from 6 to 12 months

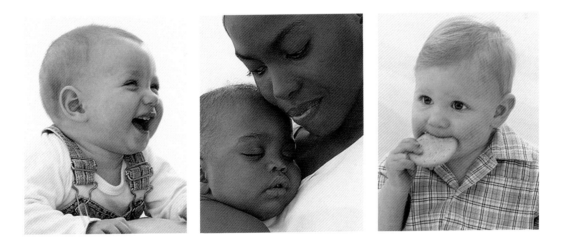

London, New York, Munich, Melbourne, Delhi

Text by Tracey Godridge
For Cora, Eden and Noah

Project editor Susannah Steel
Project art editors Claire Legemah, Glenda Fisher
Senior editor Julia North
US editors Jill Hamilton, Jane Perlmutter
Managing art editor Tracey Ward
Production controller Louise Daly
Photography Ruth Jenkinson
Art direction Sally Smallwood

First American Edition, 2002
2 4 6 8 10 9 7 5 3 1

Published in the United States by DK Publishing, Inc.,
95 Madison Avenue, New York, NY 10016

A Cataloging-in-Publication record is
availablefrom the Library of Congress
ISBN 0-7894-8445-5

Reproduced by Colourscan Overseas Pte Ltd, Singapore
Printed by Graphicom, Italy

See our complete catalog at
www.dk.com

Contents

A message to parents from Johnson & Johnson

For more than 100 years, Johnson & Johnson has been caring for babies. Our baby products help mothers and fathers soothe, comfort, and nurture a deep, loving bond with their child through everyday care.

Building on our commitment to children and families, Johnson & Johnson established the Johnson & Johnson Pediatric Institute, LLC. This unique organization promotes continued learning and research in pediatrics, infant development, and pregnancy, building programs and initiatives for professionals, parents, and caregivers that shape the future of children's health worldwide.

Through science, we continue to learn more about our youngest and their physical, cognitive, and emotional development. Parents and caregivers want advice on how to use this learning in their daily lives to complement their basic instincts to love, hold, and talk to their babies.

Good parenting is not a one-size-fits-all formula. With JOHNSON'S® *Child Development* series, we hope to support today's families with the knowledge, guidance, and understanding to help them bring forth the miracle embodied in each and every child.

The second six months

Your baby is now six months old – and he's bursting with life! Over the coming months he'll amaze you with his achievements and delight you with his love as he develops into his own unique little person.

Your baby's development

For the first six months of your baby's life, you were the center of her world: she relied on you for all her physical and emotional needs. During her second six months, however, she'll begin to develop new skills to help her extend her horizons, explore her environment, assert her own will, and discover her independence.

The wider world

Reaching her natural milestones – such as discovering how to sit, crawl, and communicate – enables your baby to really start interacting with the wider world. She can see a favorite toy and move forward to grab it. Her older brother may make a funny face to make her laugh and she can make one back! If she meets another baby she can reach out with interest toward him.

Developing independence

Watching your baby acquiring new skills is exciting, and will give you a sense of her developing independence. The fact that she can soon sit on her own, crawl happily around the floor, amuse herself with a new toy, and feed herself at the table gives you a little taste of freedom – every now and then you may even have time to sit down with a cup of coffee. A daily outing in the stroller is another step in introducing your baby to the wider world, and gives you both important "out and about" time together.

New relationships

Your baby will also become more involved and responsive with other people, especially close family members. With their instinctive sociability, babies at six months and older can start to develop a close bond with people other than their parents, such as grandparents and caregivers. This is a good time to help your baby establish separate relationships with people who will become important in her life – especially as, in a few months' time, "stranger anxiety" (pp.8–9) may make new friendships a lot harder.

Part of the family

During these next six months your baby will also really begin to enjoy her siblings, or love to watch an older toddler or child bouncing around. And as she begins to

move around herself and becomes capable of doing more things, many activities can be shared, such as singing songs together, playing clapping games, or having a game of chase (on all fours!) around the living room. Older children can also play the role of teacher for your baby. She'll love to imitate them and may try hard to look at a book like her big brother or sister, for example.

Making friends

Your friends' babies can offer similar benefits. If this is your first baby, her encounters with other babies and toddlers will probably be as a result of the friendships you have made during pregnancy and after birth. Over the next six months, your baby and your friends' babies may start to interact, gurgling at each other, touching, and trying to imitate each other's sounds and movements.

About this book

During these thrilling six months of change, your support, encouragement, and love can do more than anything else to help your baby blossom. Understanding how your baby develops is vital to helping you tune into her needs and give her what she wants.

Section 1

The first half of this book explains how your baby's development will affect both her physical and her emotional needs. For example, why does your eight-month-old keep waking at night when she previously slept through? How important is it that she moves on from purées to lumpier food at a certain age? Now that she has begun crawling, how can you keep her safe?

Being one step ahead in terms of knowing what to expect from your baby will help you understand her so that you can respond in the best and most effective way possible. And being able to meet her needs in this way will not only help her feel loved and valued but boost your confidence as a mother or father, too.

Section 2

The second half of this book contains a breakdown of each new milestone in your baby's life, and when she might be likely to reach the next stage.

Although this information is organized month by month, it's important to remember that the time-scale is flexible. All babies develop at different rates, and your baby will progress at the speed that's right for her. A certain amount of growth and development needs to take place before a new skill can be acquired by a child. So don't expect your baby to pull herself to standing, for example, before she's strong enough to support her own weight easily with her knees and hips.

Once you see your baby trying to do something new, there are lots of things you can do to try and encourage her along the way, and this section includes ideas for games and activities you can play with her. Giving your baby the right kind of stimulation at just the right time will build her confidence and self-esteem and help give her the best possible start in life.

Developing socially

As your baby enters the second half of his first year, you'll see him become more sociable and he'll reward everyone with big smiles and gurgles. Being exposed to lots of friendly faces will allow him to relax in other people's company, and help deal with the inevitable onset of separation and stranger anxiety in the next few months.

Separation and stranger anxiety

From around seven months onward, and probably for some time to come, your sociable and outgoing baby may become more clingy and be wary of people he doesn't know well. He may be reluctant to be left with anyone other than you, and even new settings may upset him. While some are more affected than others, all babies go through separation and stranger anxiety. It's a major emotional milestone and shows that your baby is growing up. For the first time he can tell the difference between familiar and unfamiliar situations. He's also beginning to realize that you and he are different people.

Child care and what your baby needs

Introducing your baby to a new babysitter or caregiver can be especially difficult when your baby is experiencing separation and stranger anxiety. But with the right person, your baby will gradually accept the situation and even benefit from having another warm and loving relationship in his life. At this age, a good babysitter or caregiver should have the following qualities:

★ Be happy to go at your baby's pace. If she forces herself on your baby, she could easily upset him.

★ Be understanding and patient. If your baby cries when you leave him, you need to feel reassured that your babysitter or caregiver won't take it personally and begin to feel inadequate.

★ Be fun and imaginative. If she knows how to distract your baby so that you can slip away peacefully, it will help both you and your baby.

★ Enjoy cuddling and chatting to your baby. Your baby still needs lots of physical affection and attention to help him feel happy and secure.

Make sure your baby feels really special. If he feels safe and well loved, his confidence will be boosted and he will cope better when you leave.

How to help

When your baby wraps his arms tightly around you, your heart will melt. But when he refuses to be put down and cries as if his heart will break if you leave the room, you may feel overwhelmed by his intense feelings. Try to remember that this is a stage that will pass.

● **Take it in stages.** Gradually realizing that you always come back when you say you will can help your baby: if you need to pop into another room, tell him where you're going and that you won't be a minute – if he cries, call to let him know you're on your way back. Also allow your baby to crawl into other rooms to give him the confidence to explore places on his own, but always follow close behind him to make sure that he stays safe.

● **Meeting new people.** Don't force your baby to be friendly – let him make eye contact in his own time. Even family members whom your baby hasn't seen for a few days may upset him without intending to.

KEEPING YOU IN HER SIGHT
Your baby's desire to be near you is a positive sign. It shows that she has developed a deep attachment to you as a parent, and to others close to her. And the more secure she feels, the faster – and more smoothly – she'll pass through this phase.

● **Giving advance warning.** When you know you have to go out, always tell your baby a little while in advance (but never more than 10 or 15 minutes beforehand or he'll forget!). This way he'll know what to expect rather than worry that you might leave him any time.

● **Getting acquainted with a caregiver.** If you have arranged for your baby to be watched by a caregiver or babysitter, give him time to become familiar with their face and begin to respond and form an attachment to them while you are still in the same room.

● **Act calmly.** When it's time to leave, give your baby a hug and a kiss goodbye and go without a fuss. If you look calm and happy, your baby will feel reassured. If your baby cries, tell him you know he'll miss you, and you'll miss him too, but you will be back shortly. Waving out of the window is a good distraction.

● **Try not to worry.** Chances are that even if your baby is in tears when you leave him, within a few minutes of your departure he'll be engaged with the person caring for him. Rather than spending your time away worrying and feeling guilty, make a quick phone call home or peep back through the window to reassure yourself that your baby is fine.

Developing personalities

Your baby is a unique individual, with her own set of fingerprints and a distinctive personality that will develop in the months and years to follow. How does this happen? Some of her traits may be inherited, but much of the way she develops will depend on her daily experiences and her interaction with you and others close to her.

Recognizing character traits

Walk into a pediatrician's office and you'll see a whole range of identifiable personalities – from cheerful and adaptable, to fretful and demanding. Some babies love to be cuddled, others will only want physical affection when it suits them. Some are sociable and daring, others are cautious and reserved. And, of course, many babies are a mixture of some or all of these characteristics.

Understanding her requirements

Your baby's character traits will become more obvious to you as she grows. Watching them unfold is not only thrilling, it also helps you tune into her needs so that you can nurture the positive sides of her personality and help her moderate other behavior. For example:

• an easy-going, placid baby may be a dream to care for, but she still needs attention and stimulation even if she doesn't always demand it.

• a shy, reserved baby needs time to adapt to new situations and people. You need to be supportive and reassuring to help her cope with experiences she might otherwise find overwhelming.

• an unsettled or demanding baby needs you to be calm and consistent, with a regular routine and lots of patience.

   At this time, all babies can be more demanding of your attention. It is important to keep in mind that your baby won't always be this needy, and that her character is still forming. From the age of six months onward, most babies are starting to settle down and become more responsive to you. The key is to try and focus on bringing out the best in your baby.

Helping her personality develop

Although your baby may be showing clear character traits at a young age, her personality is still emerging. And in the same way that her character traits affect the way you respond to her, so your responses will have an impact on her personality.

From six months old and beyond, as your baby becomes increasingly aware that she is a separate person from you, it is important to help her develop a strong sense of self. You can do this in a number of ways:

● **Show her how much you love her.** Giving your baby lots of smiles, hugs, and kisses will make her feel valued as a separate and unique individual.

● **Praise all her achievements.** Whether it's waving to you or banging two blocks together, her self-confidence will be boosted by your applause and encouragement.

● **Tune into her needs.** Knowing when she's frightened, excited, or bored, and responding accordingly, will help her feel important and loved.

● **Give her time to discover things for herself.** Letting her work hard to reach for a toy, for example, will help her develop her sense of independence as well as improving her movement control.

Putting it into practice

As you tune into her individual personality and start to encourage the positive characteristics she displays, within a few months you may begin to see your baby's developing sense of self in action as she starts to gleefully assert her will. Whether she's refusing to cooperate with you when you get her dressed or try to change her diaper, insisting that you play peekaboo again for the umpteenth time, or banging her spoon in fury because she wants to eat her food right now, you'll be left in no doubt about her likes and dislikes! But it is all these qualities – what makes her laugh and cry, her favorite foods, the games she loves – that combine together to help create her unique personality.

A question of gender

Although you may not consciously realize what you are doing, chances are that the way you care for and respond to your baby will also be affected by her sex.

Research has shown that parents of girls tend to:

★ talk gently, smile a lot, and hold them softly

★ avoid physical fun like flying them through the air

★ keep bath time quieter than with boys

★ encourage play with soft cuddly toys

★ allow them to cry when they hurt themselves and offer lots of sympathy.

On the other hand, parents of boys tend to:

★ speak loudly and hold them firmly

★ give them lots of physical stimulation – swinging them around, for example

★ encourage them to kick and splash around in the bath

★ admire their physical strength and sense of adventure

★ let them play with tough, durable toys

★ discourage any tears and sympathy when they hurt themselves.

While boys and girls are naturally different in lots of ways – girls, for example, do tend to be more sociable and less adventurous than boys, and boys are usually more physical and inquisitive than girls – the way we adults respond to them also tends to reinforce these gender differences. Tempering your behavior toward them – encouraging your boy's gentler side, or stimulating your girl's sense of independence – will begin to help eliminate any sexual stereotyping and allow your baby's own individuality to emerge.

Encouraging individuality

The way you bring up your baby will have a strong influence on his personality. And no matter what genes and personality traits are passed down your family line and inherited by your baby, he will still develop his own characteristics. But how should you encourage identical twins, or triplets, who share the same genetic makeup and the same family and experiences, to develop their own identities?

A question of genes

Every baby inherits half his genes from his mother (via the ovum) and half from his father (via the sperm). Each sperm and ovum contains a different combination of genes, which is why every child has his own unique looks and personality.

And while it is easy to see where certain individual physical characteristics come from – those dark-brown eyes are definitely his mother's, but that auburn hair must be his dad's! – what about your baby's personality? How can you tell which parts are inherited and which parts have developed over the weeks and months? You can only guess. Trying to spot any family similarities is great fun – maybe he has inherited his mother's calmness or his father's sense of humor – but because your baby is influenced by his surroundings and experiences from the moment he is born, it is impossible to know precisely which characteristics he has inherited, and which have developed over time.

Being a twin

Nurturing babies as individuals is especially important if you have twins, or even triplets. This is even more important if they are identical twins.

Identical twins develop from the same egg and are always the same sex. And because they appear so very much alike physically, it's easy to expect them to be alike emotionally and think in the same way. Treating twins as one unit rather than as two separate individuals can actually delay their physical and emotional growth, as well as slow their language and intellectual development. Thinking of your twin babies as different children and and treating them as such is vital. This will help them develop their own personalities and give them a firm emotional foundation from which to grow.

Influencing the genes

The way you react to your baby's temperament and behavior has a big influence on his developing personality. While your baby's genes may suggest that he is going to be outgoing or shy, calm, or volatile, the way you interact with him and his day-to-day experiences may or may not mean he stays this way. If you are consistently calm with an easily agitated baby, he may gradually become more relaxed. If you are supportive and reassuring with a naturally shy baby, he may, with time, become more outgoing and sociable.

Seeing twins as individuals

There are lots of practical ways of encouraging your twins' individuality, including:

- choosing names that sound very different
- not calling them "the twins" but referring to them as "the girls" or "the children." Ask family and friends to do the same, too.
- making sure you and everyone else can tell them apart from each other. You may like to paint a little fingernail on one hand each in a different color, give them different hairstyles, or even different-colored socks so that they don't get called by each other's name.
- avoiding dressing them in the same clothes
- letting them have their own selection of books, toys, and other personal items, even if it means duplicating some of them. You can identify whose is whose with their initials or name labels.

Encouraging a sense of self

There are also lots of ways of nurturing your twins' unique sense of self.

- **Spend time alone with each twin**. This can be hard, especially if you have another child or children, too. But regularly having some one-on-one time with each separate twin will make them feel loved and valued as individuals, not just as a unit.
- **Look for the unique in each twin.** Learn how to appreciate what is special about each individual child, even if it's just that one baby chuckles more when he's tickled, while the other loves bouncing on your knee.
- **Try not to compare them.** General statements that tend to compare twin siblings can sometimes become permanent labels. As they get older and more aware, such labels may actually damage their individual self-esteem and even create an unhealthy competitiveness. Always find something positive to say about each individual baby.

INDIVIDUAL IDENTITIES
Twins may be reluctant to be separated, but as they get older it is important for them to feel happy about being apart if they are to grow up secure and well balanced.

- **Introduce them to other babies.** Do this from an early age so that they feel happy in social groups. With their similarities and close physical proximity, twins often develop a special bond, which may occasionally lead them to prefer each other's company over everyone else's.

Developmental checkup for 6-9 months

During her first year your baby should have at least six main health checkups with your pediatrician, including a developmental review when she is between six and nine months old. These checkups are to ensure that your baby is progressing well. They are also a good chance for you to discuss any worries you may have (*see box*).

The timing of your baby's six to nine month checkup, and who undertakes it, will vary depending on where you live. When you go to the clinic you'll need to take your baby's medical records book, which you will have been given when your baby was born. This not only contains details of the checkup required but provides a place to have her progress recorded.

If your baby has been unwell recently, or was born premature, make sure that you let your doctor know. Illness could affect how your baby behaves at the checkup, while babies born early need this factor taken into account since it can affect their rate of progress.

Your baby's physical checkups

Your baby will have changed a lot since her last main checkup. Now she'll be babbling, sitting up, and really aware of the world around her. For this reason, your baby's development will play a larger part in her six-nine month checkup.

● **Is she growing normally?** Your baby's length, weight, and head circumference will be compared to previous measurements to make sure her growth rate is normal.

● **Is her fontanele closing?** The fontanele, or soft spot, at the front of her head will be checked. By six months it should be getting smaller, and by nine months it may even have closed.

● **Are her hips and legs okay?** Although your baby's hips and legs were checked at her six to eight week review, hip dislocation can still occur in older babies as well as in newborns.

● **Is her eyesight alright?** This will be assessed for a number of reasons, including: to make sure that she can focus clearly on an object held 10 feet (three meters) away from her; and to check that she can follow a moving object at this distance.

● **Can she hear clearly?** In order to check your baby's hearing, your pediatrician will probably shake a rattle or whisper just behind your baby's head to see if she turns around to find out where the new noise is coming from. Not all babies respond first time, especially if they are absorbed in something else, might be feeling sleepy, or have a cold. If this is the case, you will be asked back for another assessment at a later date to make sure that her hearing is fine.

- **Can she bear her own weight?** By nine months of age your baby should be strong enough to be able to take all her own weight on her feet if you hold both her hands to help her balance.
- **Can she feed herself finger food?** Your baby's hand–eye coordination and manipulation skills should be good enough at nine months for her to pick up small pieces of food and put them in her mouth.
- **Can she reach for and hold objects?**
- **Can she swap an object easily from one hand to the other?**
- **Does she look for dropped or hidden toys?**
- **Does she enjoy playing sociable games, such as peekaboo?**
- **Is she communicating with you?** You'll be asked whether your baby is babbling (making sounds such as "ba-ba," "da-da," etc.). The doctor will also watch to see if she's interested in listening to you talk, and how she manages to get your attention.

Your baby's developmental checkups

At this age, most doctors check a baby's development simply by watching the way she behaves and interacts with you, and by asking you about how she's doing at home. Questions the doctor will usually ask include the following:

- **Can she sit alone?** By nine months, your baby's balance should be good enough for her to manage sitting up unsupported.
- **Is she attempting to crawl?** Don't worry if your baby hasn't mastered crawling yet as long as she is trying to get mobile – for example, rolling over, or shuffling on her bottom to get a toy she wants that's just out of reach.

Questions for you to ask

Your baby's developmental reviews are a great chance for you to raise any concerns you may have – whether they are about your baby's health, her development, or just general parenting issues. It's a good idea to make a written note of any questions you want to ask before you go to the doctor. These may include, for example:

★ how to wean your baby from the breast or bottle onto a cup

★ how to stop night feeding

★ how to help your baby sleep though the night.

At the same time you may be given useful information by the doctor about general health and safety issues such as how to make sure your baby has a healthy diet, how to protect her against sunburn, and how to keep her safe in the car.

Keeping records

From the time he is born until he starts school, all aspects of your child's health development will be checked regularly. Keeping records is important to ensure that your baby is progressing well; it also provides a useful history of your baby's well-being. You and your pediatrician can record everything to do with your baby's health and development.

Growth charts

At every visit, including the six to nine month checkup (pp.14–15), your doctor will note your baby's weight, height, and head circumference and measure the results against a percentile chart. This information will be

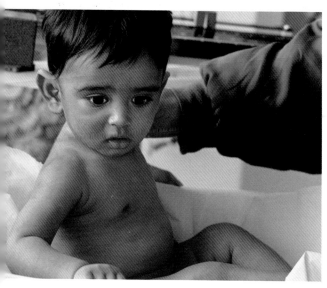

WEIGHING
During the second half of his first year your baby's weight gain will be slower than during the first half. This is perfectly normal, as are fluctuations – especially when he is unwell or going through a fussy period about eating his food.

recorded in your baby's medical records. These charts, based on statistics, show the rate at which your baby is growing. There is a separate chart for girls and boys – usually red for girls, and blue for boys! – and in each chart the middle line marks what is called the 50th percentile. This means that if you take 100 babies, 50 will be heavier and taller than the 50th line (above it) and 50 will be lighter and smaller (below it).

Plotting the measurements

Your baby's height will be plotted on one percentile chart and his length on another; all you or your doctor has to do is find the age of your baby in months at the bottom of the chart and his length or weight in inches or centimeters on the left-hand side of the chart. The spot where the age and length or weight meet is marked with a cross. Each cross is then joined up to make a curve.

What to expect

As long as your baby's chart shows that he is growing steadily, there is nothing to worry about. Most babies are on the same percentile for both their weight and height, and stay roughly on the same percentile during their first year, although there will be small fluctuations. These

Immunization schedules

Listed below are the immunizations your baby should have during the first months and years of his life, although immunization schedules do vary greatly from one country to another. It is largely down to successful immunization programs that major childhood diseases such as diphtheria and polio are now rare. But we can't forget about them – all the diseases children are vaccinated against can be dangerous, and if immunization rates fall the diseases could become common again. Some immunizations such as DTaP and Hib are available in combined forms, which means that your baby needs fewer injections. Ask your doctor.

After being immunized, your baby may appear fussed and tired, have a slight temperature, and the area where he had the injection may be red and sensitive. These are all normal reactions; treat with infant acetaminophen.

Vaccine	To protect against	Age usually given	Method
DTaP	Diphtheria, tetanus, pertussis (whooping cough)	Two, four, six, and 12–18 months	Injection
PV	Polio	Two, four, and 6–18 months, 4–6 years	Injection
Hib	Haemophilus influenza type B	Two, four, six, and 12–15 months	Injection
Hep B	Hepatitis B (if mother is negative)	Two, three, and six months	Injection
Pneumococcal (PCV)	Pneumococcal disease; can lead to meningitis, pneumonia, and ear infections	Two, four, six, and 12–15 months	Injection

Credit: American Academy of Pediatrics, Recommended childhood immunization schedule, United States, January–December 2001

fluctuations are nothing to worry about – babies can have periods of rapid growth and then slow down again for a while. Percentile charts are just guidelines, and it is the general pattern over several months that is important.

Only significant changes are cause for concern - if, for example, your baby's weight starts to fall into the lower or climb into the higher percentiles, or if there is a wide discrepancy between length and weight.

Medical history

Keeping a record of your baby's illnesses and particular treatments is useful if your doctor needs to know anything about his medical history. Faced with a sick baby, most moms feel anxious and may find it hard to rely purely on memory. Any notes you have to hand to give your doctor will help him with important information, such as which childhood illnesses your baby has already had, whether he is prone to certain kinds of illnesses, and whether he has ever suffered an allergic reaction to a certain type of medication.

Details of illness

Keep records of your child's illnesses in a notebook. Include:

- the date when your baby became ill
- the date when he recovered
- what his symptoms were
- when you went to see or called your pediatrician
- what the diagnosis was
- what instructions your pediatrician gave you
- what medication was prescribed and for how long
- if there were any side effects from the medication.

Teething

Spotting your baby's first tooth is an exciting moment. First teeth usually make an appearance between six and nine months, although some babies cut theirs as early as three months or as late as 12 months. Other babies are even born with a tooth already in place. Like lots of changes in your baby over the next few months, teething is affected by hereditary factors, and every child's circumstances are unique.

Changes in behavior

When your baby begins to teethe, don't be surprised if you notice a change in her general behavior. She may, for example, now refuse to drink from her cup, having previously delighted in the independence it gave her, or insist on being held all the time when before she was quite happy to have periods sitting and playing by herself. Pain or discomfort from teeth can temporarily affect a baby's pace of development and there may be

some regression with previously acquired skills. Once she's feeling like her old self again, your baby will quickly pick up where she left off and continue to make progress.

How her teeth grow

Most babies first start to lose their gummy grins at about six months when the bottom front teeth, known as the lower central incisors (the cutting teeth), appear. Other teeth then appear in approximately the following order: the upper central incisors come in between six and eight months and the four lateral incisors at nine months. Next come four front molars (the flat grinding teeth) between 10 and 14 months, followed by the canines (the pointed eye teeth) and the front molars at between 16 and 18 months. Your baby's back molars probably won't appear until she's nearing her second birthday. Most babies have all 20 baby teeth by the time they are two and a half.

Is she teething?

Many babies show no obvious signs of teething, and you may be taken by surprise when her first tooth pops up through her gum. Other babies, however, are fretful and irritable, sometimes for a couple of months before a new tooth appears. It can be difficult knowing whether this unhappiness is being caused by something else such as illness (*see below*). But common signs of teething may include one, or all, of the following:

- swollen, reddened gums
- excessive drooling
- an inflamed cheek
- mild cough
- low-grade fever
- biting down on anything she can get in her mouth.

Teething and illness

Complaints, such as those listed below, are often blamed on teething, but should be treated as separate illnesses.

- **High temperatures.** A fever of 100.4˚F (38˚C) or higher for more than 24 hours could be a sign of infection. Give your baby infant acetaminophen. If the fever continues for more than one day see your doctor.
- **Diarrhea.** This is serious since babies can become dehydrated very quickly. Give her plenty of fluids, and if it continues for more than 24 hours call your doctor.
- **Earache.** If your baby is tugging at her ear, she may have an infection that could cause damage to her ear. It can also become painful very quickly. Call your doctor.
- **Chest infections.** A mild cough is common when teething, since the excessive saliva produces extra mucus. If your baby has a temperature and has difficulty breathing, she may have a chest infection. Call your doctor.

Caring for her teeth

As your baby's teeth appear, start cleaning them twice a day with a child's soft toothbrush and add a pea-sized blob of toothpaste when she's able to spit out. If she won't open her mouth for a toothbrush, use a clean finger. Encourage her to spit out, not swallow, the toothpaste. You should also avoid giving her sugary snacks, sweets, and drinks in between meals, and never give her sugared pacifiers, fruit juice, or honey drinks at bedtime.

Soothing your baby

If your baby is cranky, she'll need soothing. Check first that there isn't an underlying cause such as illness (*see below left*). Otherwise, the following suggestions may help:

★ Something cold to chew on – teething rings, any clean, age-appropriate toy such as a rattle, or even a frozen bagel may all help, but remember never to leave your baby alone with food in case she chokes.

★ A gum massage: pressing down on her gums with a clean finger may give her relief.

★ Teething gels. Available from your local pharmacist, these gels contain a mild local anesthetic that can temporarily ease the pain, although they may quickly wash out of your baby's mouth.

★ Lots to drink, especially if your baby is drooling a lot and needs the extra fluids. Try diluted fruit juice.

★ An occasional dose of sugar-free infant acetaminophen for temperatures of 100.4˚F (38˚C) or higher.

Healthy eating

As your baby learns how to sit up properly, grip a spoon, and discover how to feed himself over the next few months, he will become an active participant in family meals. And he'll love it when you all eat together. Mealtimes will also become easier for you as he starts to enjoy the same food as everyone else.

The number of foods you can now give your baby is rapidly expanding. It's also a good time to set healthy eating patterns that will benefit him for the rest of his life. Advice on which foods are suitable can sometimes change, so check also with your pediatrician.

Eating for healthy growth

As your baby enters the second half of his first year, he should have two or three meals a day in addition to breast or formula milk, which is still part of his main diet. He can try most family foods, if they do not contain added salt and are not too sweet. Introduce them one at a time to check that he has no allergies or sensitivities.

Once your baby has been on solids for a couple of months, move on from purées to mashed or chopped foods with more texture. From nine to 10 months old, he should be happy to eat family meals such as chicken casserole or macaroni and cheese as long as there is no added salt, but remember that if three meals a day is not possible then eating little and often can be just as good.

Encouraging healthy eating for life

One of the best ways you can help your baby to grow up fit and healthy – and stay that way – is to encourage him to develop healthy eating habits now.

● Introduce variety in the form of different tastes, colors, and textures. This will keep him interested in his

THE RIGHT DIET

The key to eating well at this age is to make sure that your baby has a wide variety of foods – cooked and uncooked – from each of the four main food groups (see box), and nutritious snacks to keep his energy levels up.

The right foods to give

Your baby should have at least one portion of fish, meat, egg, lentils, or beans every day, since these are the best sources of protein and iron. By the time your baby is six months old, the reserves of iron with which he was born are used up, and milk alone will not provide all his daily requirements. Give your baby food from each of the four main food groups every day:

★ **Dairy products** such as cheese, yogurt, or whole milk cottage cheese. Until he is 12 months old, your baby still needs about 17-20fl oz (500-600ml) of breast or formula milk a day. Although he can't have cow's milk as a drink until he is one year old, you can now start to add cow's milk in small quantities to a cheese sauce, for example, or to his breakfast cereal.

★ **Carbohydrates** such as potatoes, bread, rice, noodles, pasta, couscous, and breakfast cereals. Foods containing gluten are now fine to try.

★ **Fruit and vegetables** – increase the variety.

★ **Meat and meat alternatives.** Start your baby off with some soft, white flaked fish such as cod or haddock, or some well-minced chicken or lamb. He will also enjoy small quantities of well-cooked lentils or beans. Eggs are okay if they are also well cooked: try a hard-boiled egg, or strips of cooled omelette. Start by giving him the yolk of the egg only, since it is less likely to cause an allergy. Many nutritionists recommend cooked egg white only after your baby is one year old.

food; even small babies get bored with the same food every day. Don't worry if he leaves something new: babies' tastes are fickle and he may try it again tomorrow.

● **Praise him when he eats well.** If you want your baby to love natural, healthy foods, make sure he's offered plenty of it, and give him lots of praise when he eats it.

● **Avoid sugary "treats."** Sugar, which suppresses the appetite and is harmful to teeth, can easily be avoided altogether for your baby's first year. If your baby gets used to the idea that sugary foods are a special treat

now, he'll quickly think they are a good thing – and studies show that babies who are exposed to sugar early on develop a stronger taste for it than those who aren't.

● **Offer healthy snacks.** Babies use up lots of energy, and once they are on the move they can quickly become hungry again. Boost your baby's energy with nutritious snacks such as little pieces of fruit (fresh or dried), natural yogurt, rice cakes or breadsticks.

● **Avoid fast food.** Take healthy foods with you for mealtimes when you are out and about with your child so that you don't have to rely on fast food restaurants; french fries, hamburgers, hot dogs, and soft drinks are all high in fats, salt, and sugar and may contain lots of additives, which should be avoided.

Foods to avoid

At this age there are still certain foods that are not suitable for your baby to try. These include:

● **Salt, sugar, and honey** (sweeten desserts with mashed banana instead).

● **Sugary fruit drinks and diet drinks.** If you want to offer your baby an alternative to milk or water at mealtimes, give him not more than 4fl oz (120ml) diluted, unsweetened fruit juice a day.

● **Foods that carry a high risk of food poisoning.** These include mold-ripened cheese (such as blue cheese) and soft-boiled eggs.

● **Nuts.** Avoid all nuts and nut products containing peanuts, especially if your family is known to have a history of allergies.

● **Low-fat and high-fiber foods.** Babies need more calories and less bulk to give them the energy they need to grow.

● **Foods that present a choking hazard.** These include whole grapes, nuts, popcorn, large pieces of apple or raw carrot, uncooked peas, and celery. Even hamburgers and hot dogs are a risk unless they are well chopped up.

Learning to eat

At around six or seven months old, your baby's developmental progress means that mealtimes are becoming a very different affair. Now she can sit up unaided you'll need to invest in a high chair. She'll enjoy watching you get her food ready, but if she can't wait try keeping her busy with a selection of toys on her tray attachment.

Learning to chew

You need to start introducing your baby to lumpier foods if you want her to develop chewing skills, but don't imagine she can cope with a steak just because her first teeth have appeared! She'll still use her gums to chew for a while yet and needs her food lightly mashed until she is about one year old – although softer food such as bread or pasta can be left whole if you wish.

Some babies don't take kindly to finding lumps in their previously puréed food, and may react by spitting them out. If your baby does this, don't rush her: learning how to chew is quite a difficult exercise, especially since she has only known how to suck until now. Instead, offer her finger foods (*see right*) as soon as she can hold them to help her practice chewing and explore new textures.

Introducing finger foods

By seven months, your baby will probably be eager to start finger foods. Her hand–eye coordination has improved to such an extent that she can now pick up

CHEWING PRACTICE
Learning how to chew is important not only because it will increase the range of foods your baby can eat, but also because it helps him practice moving his mouth and tongue, ready to learn how to talk.

a piece of food and put it to her mouth, albeit none too tidily. For now she'll hold the food in her fist and work hard to push the last messy mouthful in with the flat of her hand. By nine months, however, she has better control of her thumb and forefinger, and with this pincer grip she can pick up tiny pieces of food such as raisins or peas.

First finger foods for your baby are those that can be gummed to a soft consistency for swallowing or that will dissolve in the mouth without chewing. Always cut food into manageable chunks and don't offer too much at a time: she'll either try to stuff it in all at once or sweep all of it onto the floor. Foods to try include:

- bread, rice cakes, toast
- tiny cubes of hard cheese
- chunks of soft fruit such as banana, peach, or melon
- small pieces of cooked carrot, broccoli and cauliflower (cut the stalks off), sweet potato
- well-cooked pasta - cut up as necessary
- scrambled egg.

Once your baby's front molars appear – from about 10 months onward – you can offer her harder, firmer food such as pieces of apple or small pieces of chicken. And remember always to stay with your baby when she's eating, in case of choking.

Trying to self-feed

Babies like to try feeding themselves with a spoon from an early age. Until she's nine months or so, your baby will probably keep overturning the spoon before it reaches her mouth, so it is worth remembering these points.

- Self-feeding is an important step forward and boosts your baby's confidence and independence.
- She needs lots of practice, which means it's important to ignore the mess! Rather than be tempted to take over, put a mat under her high chair to catch spillages and dropped food, and remind yourself that this phase passes.
- Make sure she's getting enough food in her mouth by

Weaning to a cup

This is a good time to introduce a two-handled cup in place of a bottle or breastfeed at lunchtime. You'll have to show your baby how to move it to her mouth and tip the liquid out, and it will be a while before she's happy to take all her daily milk quota this way. Be patient - moving off her bottle will help improve her speech development, and drinks from a cup spend less time in contact with her teeth, so it's better for her dental health. It's also beneficial to wean your baby off her bottle earlier rather than later so that she doesn't become attached to it as a security object.

slipping in mouthfuls of food with your own spoon in between her attempts. Later on you may only need to help with loading up her spoon.

When she won't eat

There will be times when your baby rejects her food. It may be that she just isn't hungry today, she's teething, or that there are distractions in the room. Never force-feed your child, and avoid making mealtimes a battle. She may play with her food, which is perfectly normal, but if she is bored and does not want any more, take it away and try again later. However, talk to your doctor if you are at all concerned about your baby's diet.

Sleeping

Sleep – or lack of it – is a major issue for most parents. But sleep is vital for babies, too, so that they can grow and develop properly: it is during sleep that growth hormones are released and new cells grow fastest. Not enough sleep can make an otherwise happy baby fussy, difficult, and maybe less responsive.

By the time your baby is six months old he should be able to sleep through the night. If he isn't sleeping through, there are steps you can take to help give you both a good night's rest. But that doesn't mean your baby will go through every night without a problem: as he experiences separation anxiety (pp.8–9), for example, he may start waking again and looking for you for comfort.

How much sleep does he need?

While newborn babies tend to sleep for as many as 18 hours out of 24, by the time they are six months old many babies need 12 to 14 hours sleep in a 24-hour period, including a couple of one- or two-hour naps. However, this arrangement may not last long. Within a few months your baby may drop one daytime nap – usually the mid-morning rest – while a few babies decide to drop both naps and want to stay awake all day!

Are daytime naps important?

Daytime naps provide welcome and much-needed free time for you. The more rested your baby is, the happier he'll be during the day and easier to settle down at night.

Some babies, however, are naturally more wakeful than others. If your baby seems content without his regular morning or afternoon nap and settles easily at night, then the chances are he's found a balance that works well for him.

But if he seems tired and fussy, yet resists a daytime nap, it may be that he just finds life around him too exciting and doesn't want to leave it even for a second. As his daytime nap draws near, try not to overstimulate him. Keep him calm and quiet and try putting him down

SLEEPING PRACTICE
Encouraging your baby to drift off to sleep in her crib on her own helps her establish good sleeping patterns.

to sleep before he becomes overtired. Make sure the room is dark and quiet with nothing to distract him. If he still resists, and you're faced with the prospect of dealing with a cranky baby for the rest of the day, you could try taking him out for a walk or a drive in the car. Lots of babies nod off when they are on the move, and even a 20-minute nap in his stroller or car seat will refresh him for the rest of the day.

When will he sleep through the night?

Every new parent is desperate for this moment to arrive! While, very occasionally, some newborn babies will give their parents an unbroken night after six to eight weeks, most won't sleep for more than five hours or so at a stretch until they are over three months old. But by the time babies are six months old – when they no longer need a night feeding (*see box*) – they should be able to sleep through the night for anything up to 11 or 12 hours.

However, even though your baby may be physically ready to sleep through the night, he may still find it hard. This may be because he is ill or teething, or experiencing separation anxiety. But often babies wake in the night simply because of their sleep pattern. During a normal night your baby will alternate between periods of deep sleep and light sleep. During these lighter sleeps – which can occur five or six times in a night – it's not unusual for babies to wake up and open their eyes, and even cry out if they can't see or feel you.

Settling back to sleep

Babies who depend on being nursed, rocked, or cuddled to sleep at bedtime will find it especially hard to settle themselves back down again if they wake during these lighter sleeping patterns. However, if you have established a good bedtime routine for your baby (*pp.26–27*), and he is used to settling himself down, he should quickly fall back into a deep sleep pattern again.

Feeding at night

By the time your baby is six months old, he should be able to sleep happily through the night if he is thriving and is established in a good routine (*see left*). If he is still waking and demanding a feeding, it's more likely to be out of habit or for comfort than because he's hungry, especially if you've recently started to wean him. At this age there is no physical reason for feeding your baby during the night.

Breastfed babies, however, find it particularly hard to give up nighttime cuddling. One solution is to ask your partner to try and settle your baby back to sleep when your baby wakes. If he can't smell your breast milk, he's more likely to drop off again. It may take a while but eventually he'll stop waking altogether.

Bedtime routines

You can avoid many sleep problems by helping your baby develop good sleeping habits. Even if it's been hard to get her into a good nighttime routine when she was younger, six months is not too late to start. And although illness, or even a change of environment, may unsettle her, once she's recovered or you are back in familiar surroundings, your baby should soon settle back into her old routine.

There are several methods you can try to help your baby get to sleep, and encourage her to learn how to sleep through the night without needing attention from you.

Follow a bedtime routine

The first step to helping your baby sleep well at night is to make sure she has a regular bedtime routine. By the age of six months she has a greater understanding of the world, and is starting to recognize her daily rituals.

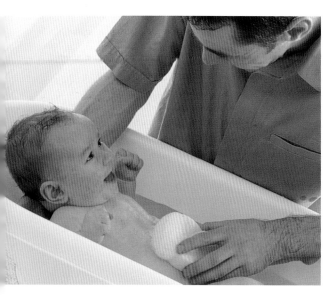

If you follow the same routine every night she'll quickly know what to expect and will soon understand that when it's nighttime it's a time to sleep, not play. Lots of parents start the bedtime routine with a warm, relaxing bath followed by a bedtime story, final feeding, teeth-brushing, and into bed. The key is to help your baby unwind, so avoid any stimulating activities.

Let her cuddle a comfort

Now your baby can roll over unaided, you may like to put her to sleep with a special comfort blanket, a muslin square, or a soft toy that meets all the required safety standards – but make sure that she can't be smothered by the toy. If a favorite teddy bear or something similar is waiting in bed for her every night, she'll quickly associate it with going to sleep. After a while, if she wakes in the night, the teddy bear's comforting presence may help her drop off again. Try cuddling the teddy bear yourself so that it smells of you, then she'll feel like she has a little piece of you with her during the night.

BATH TIME BONDING
Bath time is an important opportunity for a mom or dad to spend intimate time with their baby as they settle him down ready for bedtime.

Say goodnight while she's awake

Rocking, cuddling, or feeding a baby to sleep are major causes of sleep problems. Although it's tempting to let your baby fall asleep in your arms, this won't help her learn how to drop off to sleep again on her own when she wakes in the night. The key to developing a good sleeping pattern is to put her to bed when she's calm but still awake, give her a kiss goodnight, and leave the room.

Let her cry for a while

Most babies, especially those who are used to dropping off in a parent's arms, have trouble sleeping this way to begin with. If your baby cries out as you leave the room, try not to go back immediately. She needs a chance to cry, stop crying, and then lie there until sleep comes. When her crying sounds more desperate, go back, kiss her, tell her she's okay, and then leave again. You may have to do this repeatedly over several hours before your baby finally drops off. But it's worth persevering now, and for the next few nights. By the sixth or seventh night, most babies will learn that they are fine without you and discover that they can get themselves to sleep.

If she wakes in the night...

It can be much harder to stay calm if your baby wakes in the night. Sometimes rocking or feeding her back to sleep will seem like the fastest and easiest option, but this will prolong – not solve – the problem of nighttime waking. Instead, resolve to follow the same technique as before: go to her, check she's safe, kiss her, and reassure her that she's okay before leaving the room again. At six months old, your baby should be secure enough in your love for her to accept being left on her own. Although you'll find it emotionally and physically exhausting initially, remember that it is worth persevering! For most babies, it doesn't take more than a few nights to break the night-waking habit.

Into a separate room

Most parents like having their baby sleep in the same room as themselves – a practice that is commonplace around the world – and some medical experts agree that this is a good idea.

Once a baby is in the second half of her first year, she can make the move into a separate room if you wish. At this age babies can be easily disturbed while they sleep and may wake up when you come to bed or if you cough or turn over in the night. At this age a baby will also be able to keep herself awake if she's been disturbed, something that she couldn't do when she was younger.

If you do want to move your baby into another room, choose a time when she isn't having to cope with many other changes, such getting used to a new babysitter. Also, if she's experiencing separation anxiety it would be a good option to keep her with you in your room until she's settled again.

Communication

From the day your baby is born, he is communicating with you. Initially this is just by crying; later by smiling too, and from six months old onward he'll use a whole range of signs and gestures. It will be many months yet before your baby can actually say his first words, but that isn't going to stop him from expressing himself!

It is also the case that your baby doesn't need to know how to talk in order to understand what you say to him. In fact, a baby's understanding of language naturally develops faster than his ability to use it.

Understanding first

Babies learn how to talk at such different rates that their receptive language – how well a baby understands what is said to them – is a much better sign of the progress they are really making.

You can see this in lots of different ways. First you may notice your child turn to you when he hears his name. Then by around nine months, for example, you'll notice that he is beginning to recognize lots of words that name familiar people or objects, such as "cup" or "teddy bear." He'll laugh in the right places when you sing certain songs, look for his cup when you ask him where it is, and follow simple commands such as "Kiss mommy"

Some babies do say their first words before their first birthday (and these are usually recognizable only by their family!), but many children don't utter any

PREPARING TO TALK
By the end of his first year, your baby will be getting ready to talk – and the more you respond to him as though he is speaking, the more you'll stimulate his desire to communicate.

understandable words until they are 13 months old or so. Some children are still making themselves understood with signs and gestures well into their second year. As long as your baby seems to understand what you are saying, the chances are his speech will develop normally.

Using signs and gestures

As your baby's understanding of language is developing, so, too, is his ability to express himself with signs and gestures - another important stage in language development. He loves communicating with you, and is very creative in finding ways of letting you know what he wants. For example:

• from around seven months he may open and shut his hand when he wants something, and shake his head or push you away if you are doing something he doesn't like. Watch his face, too: his expressions will let you know if he's annoyed, happy, or frightened.

• from around nine months old he may start pointing at what he wants, wave goodbye to you, and lift his arms in the air to show he wants to be picked up.

• from around 10 months he may be able to follow simple questions such as "Do you want a drink?" and respond by shaking or nodding his head.

Though these signs and gestures are a stopgap until your baby learns how to talk, it's important to try and decipher them and show that you understand. Seeing you respond correctly fills him with confidence, develops his trust in you, and encourages his desire to communicate.

From first sounds to first words

As with all milestones, babies develop language skills at different rates, but their steps on the language ladder will usually progress in the same order.

• babbling is one of the first major steps, and usually starts at around six months old when babies gain control of their tongue, lips, and the palate of their mouth. Your

The importance of hearing

Being able to hear properly is vital for a baby's speech development since it encourages imitation, which in turn stimulates language skills. You'll notice that your baby's hearing is fine if the following occur:

★ by six or seven months he babbles, tries to imitate sounds, and turns to hear your voice across a room

★ by nine months he listens carefully to familiar sounds such as a dog barking, or the doorbell ringing

★ by one year he is responding when you say "No" or "Bye-bye."

Even partial hearing loss – caused, for example, by repeated ear infections – can interfere with speech development. If you are concerned about your baby's hearing, speak to your pediatrician, who will be monitoring his reflexes and hearing ability. Check, too, when your baby should have his hearing screened.

baby will discover his consonants first, and usually utter sounds such as "ba" or "da."

• once your baby can control his sounds well enough he'll have great fun repeating them over and over again, for example, "ba-ba-ba" or "da-da-da."

• at around eight months old he'll be producing double consonants that sound like real words - such as "ba-ba" or "da-da" (much to his father's delight!).

• between 10 and 12 months old, your baby will be stringing sounds together and using intonation in a way that sounds like real speech.

Eventually your baby's experiments with sounds will help him utter his first words - usually around his first birthday. But don't be surprised if he is only understood by you and other close family members who are familiar with the routines of his life and the words associated with them. These often aren't real words, but if you recognize what he wants and repeat the correct word back to him he will eventually begin to say the word properly.

Learning to talk

You will be thrilled to hear your baby's coos and gurgles turn into words – a huge milestone for her. Learning to talk helps her discover about the world around her, as well as bringing her closer to you. And while language learning is built in – babies are natural communicators and imitators – the part you play is crucial. With your help your baby discovers that, not only is talking important, it's fun too.

What to expect

From six months onward your baby will start to make an incredible range of sounds and over the following months her happy babbling will start to resemble more and more the pattern, tone, and pitch of adult speech.

By the end of this year some babies may even be saying their first "words," such as "gog" for dog, or "dat" for cat. Most children, however, won't master all their spoken consonants until they are three or four years old, and some not until later.

Don't be surprised if, after getting off to a flying start, your baby doesn't learn any more new words for a while. It can take up to three or four months after their first few spoken words for babies to acquire many more words. This may be especially true if, at the same time as learning to talk, your baby is busy trying to master other skills such as walking.

Developing at different rates

If your baby has older brothers or sisters, you may find that she learns to talk later than your other children. First children often do best as they have lots of one-to-one attention: mom and dad have more time to encourage them and listen to them. And although second or third

children might hear lots of chat going on around them, they may have little chance to practice their own talking – especially if siblings try to translate for them! For this reason it is important to make special time alone for you and your baby.

Ways to help

Every time you talk to your baby she'll be soaking up new information about language, and if you talk in a way that makes it easier for her to listen and learn then you'll make the most of your time together.

- **Chat away.** Whatever you are doing with your baby, one of the best ways of helping her speech improve is by talking to her about your activity. Whether it is cooking her meal or changing her diaper, describe and show her what you are doing.
- **Give her a chance to respond.** Conversation is a two-way process and your baby will love taking turns with you, so remember to pause and wait for her "reply" when you are talking to her.
- **Keep it simple.** Use short, simple sentences and try not to speak too fast. Your baby needs time to understand what you are saying and will miss anything that you say quickly.

At this age she's fascinated by lots of everyday objects such as the kettle or washing machine.

● **Repeat correctly.** If she has begun to say sounds such as "wa-wa" for water or "nana" for banana, build her confidence by using the correct word ("Would you like some water?" or "Here's your banana") to show her that you know what she's saying. Eventually she'll learn from you how to say the word correctly.

● **Play games together.** Action songs, peekaboo, and clapping games are great fun for your baby - she'll also love anticipating what comes next and the repetition will help her learn familiar words.

First books

Your baby may be too young to concentrate on real stories but looking at books together is invaluable for helping her communication skills. Try to find time every day for sitting and reading quietly together. Point at the pictures to encourage your baby to look too. Use lots of emphasis and exclamation to hold her attention.

● **Use lots of expression and emphasis.** This will add interest for your baby, especially if you exaggerate your expression sometimes for fun and use humor.

● **Be consistent.** Try to use the same words for the same objects – using "glass" one day and "cup" the next will only confuse her.

● **Help her listen.** Your baby learns to listen better if she has no distractions, so cut out any background noise.

● **Follow her lead.** When you see your baby looking with interest at something or pointing, tell her what it is.

Choosing books

When choosing books, look for:

★ sturdy board books that will survive chewing, throwing, and tearing; vinyl books are particularly good for bath time

★ large illustrations or photographs that are bright and bold

★ realistic, recognizable pictures of animals and objects

★ books that will help your baby learn to make animal noises

★ simple rhymes or one-word-per-page books

★ activity books such as "touch and feel" books to help your baby learn about texture, or books that encourage games such as peekaboo.

Safety

As your baby becomes more active, you'll need to be increasingly aware of his safety. As soon as he can roll himself over, for example, he risks falling off the changing table. Then once he starts moving he can reach dangerous places, open forbidden cabinets, even touch and taste things that could harm him.

Young babies are naturally driven to explore the world around them, yet they have no sense of the potential dangers of their environment. And although your baby will start to recognize the word "no" at this age, you can't rely on him remembering what it is he can and can't do.

Your baby needs space and a sense of freedom to stimulate his development – so being overprotective in order to avoid accidents isn't the answer. Instead:
- provide a safe environment for him to explore
- be aware of potential problems to prevent accidents before they happen

- supervise him all the time; babies should never be left alone unless they are asleep in a crib or safe in a playpen
- get down on the floor to play with your baby – this will give you the best chance of seeing what's safe, and what isn't, in your home.

Around the home
- install stair gates if your baby shows signs of crawling
- use antislam devices on doors to avoid crushed fingers
- avoid using a baby walker – your child could tip over
- install window locks
- use a five-point harness to keep him in his high chair
- keep any furniture he could climb on away from windows
- install corner guards on any sharp corners on cabinets and table edges
- check that there is no furniture your baby could pull over on top of himself
- check banisters and railings on landings or balconies to make sure he can't fall through, over, or under them
- check floors regularly for dangerously small items such as buttons, batteries, loose coins, or safety pins
- keep matches and lighters out of reach and out of sight
- cover electrical outlets with heavy furniture or with safety outlet covers
- install smoke detectors and check batteries every week.

Hygiene

★ replace or rinse any toy, food, or cup that your baby has dropped on the street

★ don't let your baby eat food he's dropped in the bathroom, puddles, or other damp or wet surfaces

★ don't let him eat something he mouthed and then left lying around for more than an hour or so

★ keep trash cans and pet food well out of your baby's reach.

In the kitchen

• store sharp implements well out of reach

• never leave hot drinks on tables or on the floor, and don't use tablecloths – your baby could tug on it and pull hot objects onto himself

• never hold a hot drink if you are carrying your baby, and watch for him crawling if you walk with a hot drink

• always supervise your baby when he is eating or drinking, to prevent him from choking

• use back burners on the stove and turn pan handles inward and out of reach – or use a pan guard

• avoid trailing electrical cords

• be aware that oven doors and radiators get very hot

• use safety catches on cupboards and keep cupboards that contain household cleaners and cleaning fluids locked

• cover refrigerated, cooked food, and do not reheat it.

In the bathroom

• never leave your baby unsupervised in the bath since young children can drown in only a few inches of water

• use a non-slip mat in the bath

• turn on the cold water first when running the bath and test the water before putting your child in

• keep your baby away from the faucet or wrap a washcloth around it and turn it off tightly

• turn the thermostat on your hot water heater to 120°F (48°C) to avoid scalding water

• lock medicines and razors out of reach in a cupboard

• keep the toilet seat down and remove the toilet brush.

In the bedroom

• once your baby can stand, make sure that there are no toys in his crib he could use to climb out

• keep his crib well away from the window

• once he can get on all fours, remove hanging mobiles

• never leave him alone on a changing table.

In the living areas

• always use fireguards around fires and heaters and make sure the guard is firmly fixed to the wall

• clear away leftover alcoholic drinks.

Out and about

• keep garden tools and chemicals safely locked away

• always use a harness in the carrriage/stroller

• remove any poisonous plants from your garden

• never leave your baby alone with or near water.

SAFETY COMES FIRST
Your baby will find all sorts of ways to investigate the world around him. Ensure that you don't leave anything dangerous on low surfaces, such as cups of hot coffee, that could spill and hurt him.

Massaging your baby

When your baby is born, the first thing you instinctively do is lovingly touch her. Physical contact, whether it's cuddling, stroking, kissing, or rocking, comes naturally and helps you develop a close relationship with your baby. It's also vital for her emotional well-being, showing that you love her and building her sense of self-worth.

Lots of mothers and fathers use baby massage to enhance their relationship with their baby. It is a wonderful way of expressing your feelings while fulfilling your baby's emotional need for skin-to-skin contact. But massage has physical benefits too, and can be used to ease lots of minor baby complaints.

Good for your baby

Massage has lots of emotional and physical benefits for your baby, including:

★ helping develop a close and trusting relationship with you

★ calming her when she's fretful – massage reduces the circulation of the stress hormone cortisol in the bloodstream

★ increasing her sense of well-being - massage also stimulates endorphins, which can lift your baby's mood

★ easing gas and constipation – stroking her tummy can help disperse trapped air

★ releasing tension caused by, for example, teething

★ relaxing arm and leg muscles and helping your baby become more mobile.

Baby massage can also be calming and relaxing for you, and knowing that your touch is comforting your baby can make you feel happy and confident as a parent.

When to do it

The best times for a massage include:

● between meals – if your baby has just eaten she'll feel uncomfortable during a massage, and if she is hungry she won't feel settled

● last thing at night after her bath – she'll be naturally relaxed and responsive

● when there are no other distractions – if the house is quiet and you are not expecting visitors, you'll be able to focus on your baby without interruption.

Don't massage your baby if she is sick, she obviously doesn't want to be massaged, or if she's just been immunized – the area of the injection may still be sore.

How to begin

● **Make sure the room is warm,** with no distractions

● **Wash your hands** and dry them thoroughly, and take off any jewelry

● **Make sure your hands are warm;** rub them together first if they feel cold to the touch

● **Use a specially formulated baby oil or lotion** that is labeled as 100 percent safe. Don't use any products containing arachis oil since this contains peanut oil and may cause a reaction

● **Undress your baby** and lie her down on a soft, warm towel on your lap or on the floor.

Head and face

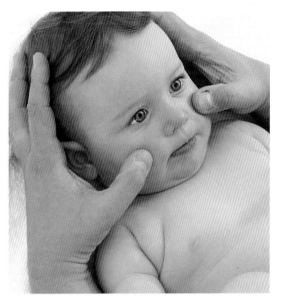

2 Gently massage her forehead, working from the center out and moving over the eyebrows and cheeks toward her ears.

1 Stroking and kissing your baby's face helps release tension. Try using your thumbs to make smiles on her upper and lower lips. Use a circular motion on her crown and then stroke down the sides of her face.

Arms and hands

2 Open one of her hands gently and rub it between your palms, then massage her palm and the back of her hand with your thumb and index fingers.

3 Spread her fingers and thumb, and one by one pull each finger gently through your thumb and forefinger. Then repeat with her other hand.

1 Massage one arm at a time. Stroke down her arm to her fingertips, then using your finger and thumb gently squeeze all along her arm, starting at the top.

Tummy

1 Place both hands in the center of your baby's chest and push gently out toward the sides, following your baby's rib cage. Without lifting your hands, bring them back round in a heart-shaped motion to the center.

2 Gently stroke her tummy using one hand in a circular clockwise motion, then walk your fingertips along her tummy from left to right.

Legs

1 As with your baby's arms, massage one leg at a time. Work from the thigh down, gently squeezing as you go.

2 Finish by gently pulling her whole leg and foot through your hands.

Feet

1 Gently knead and rub the top of each foot and roll each toe between your forefinger and thumb, separating her toes.

2 Use your thumb to rub the sole of her foot. Finish by gently pulling each toe with your fingers.

How babies learn

Over the next few months your baby is going to learn an astonishing amount. She will discover how to sit, crawl, and maybe walk, how to pick up a small object, how to recognize her family, point to what she needs, or make you laugh – and that's just for starters!

How babies learn skills

Your baby's mastery of her physical and mental skills is staggering, especially when you think how she started life – as a tiny bundle only just starting to gain a sense of herself and the world around her. So how do these incredible changes take place?

Genetics will play a part in how your baby develops, but much of her progress will also depend on the kind of stimulation and attention that she receives from you. From the moment of her birth she is absorbing information from the world around her, and in particular from the people closest to her. In a way, you are your baby's first teacher. This isn't as overwhelming as it sounds, since

your baby's natural way of learning is through play and exploration: if she shakes a rattle and discovers that it makes a fantastic noise, she's learning about cause and effect; when she tries to crawl over a mountain of cushions you've built for her she's finding out how to balance and coordinate her limbs; and when she listens to you sing a nursery rhyme she's starting to understand the basis of language development.

Encouraging your baby

How is your baby motivated? Again, it's partly a built-in drive to discover and learn. But your encouragement and support is also incredibly important. When, for example, she eventually manages to wave goodbye as a friend leaves, it's your delight and praise that boosts her sense of achievement, and convinces her that learning is fun.

Taking your lead from your baby is key to motivating her. When she's ready to try a new challenge, you'll see the signs. Understanding how and when your baby develops can help you prepare for each stage and be ready with the right kind of games and activities to stretch her and fulfil her needs. In fact, making sure her family environment is fun and stimulating is one of the most valuable things you can do for her.

Playing with your baby also brings you closer together and helps develop your baby's self-esteem and sense of security, proving that you love her unconditionally for who she is, not just what she can do.

6–12 months: your baby's milestones

Your baby will master lots of new skills and reach many important milestones over the next few months. It's important to remember, however, that while each baby will reach all of the following milestones, the time it takes to reach them will vary from baby to baby. After all, every baby develops differently.

If you ever become concerned about your baby's development, speak to your doctor – although, chances are, your baby will be progressing perfectly normally.

Movement milestones

By 12 months she will probably:
- sit unsupported
- crawl, or similar
- pull herself up to standing
- cruise, holding onto furniture
- stand momentarily without support
- maybe walk two or three steps on her own.

Hand and finger milestones

By 12 months she will probably:
- bang two blocks together
- feed herself finger foods
- put objects in a container and take them out again
- let go of objects in her hand when she wants to

- point with her finger
- use the pincer grip (hold a tiny object with her forefinger and thumb).

Social and emotional milestones

By 12 months she will probably:
- cry when you leave her
- cling to you if strangers directly approach her
- understand the meaning of "no"
- play jokes
- enjoy imitating people.

Language milestones

By 12 months she will probably:
- babble
- listen carefully to you when you talk to her
- respond to simple commands
- recognize her name and other familiar words
- use gestures such as shaking her head for "no"
- try to imitate words.

Intellectual milestones

By 12 months she will probably:
- find hidden objects easily
- explore objects in different ways (e.g. banging, throwing, dropping)
- understand cause and effect (when she shakes her rattle, it makes a noise)
- start to understand how objects are used (drink from a cup, brush her hair, listen into a telephone).

Some babies may also be able to stack blocks, for example, or say "mama" or "dada" with meaning. But these milestones aren't just about achievements – they are also about helping ensure your baby's healthy emotional and social development.

6 to 7 months

Over halfway through her first year of life, and your baby is beginning to take a greater interest in the world around her. Now that she can sit upright she has a new perspective on her environment; she is also more sociable, remembers day-to-day routines, and is developing a true sense of herself as a unique person.

Physical development

Constantly exercising her body over the last few months has helped your baby develop her muscles, balance, and control.

Grabbing toys

Once she learns how to sit upright (*see box, right*) and no longer needs her arms to keep herself supported, your baby will be working hard to grab anything nearby that excites her, twisting around and stretching forward. Make sure there are always some toys, safe household objects, or baby books nearby to keep her interested – but don't expect too much. Her concentration skills are still developing and even something she has never seen before will only hold her attention for a few minutes.

Hand–eye coordination

As her grip develops, your baby will be able to hold objects more firmly and steadily, turn them over to have a good look at them and then put them in her mouth, pass them from one hand to the other, and even bang two objects together.

As her hand–eye coordination improves she'll be grabbing a spoon as soon as it's in sight, and probably overturning it before it reaches her mouth. You may like to try offering her a two-handled cup to drink from. Before too long, she may be drinking from it herself. You may also want to start offering her finger foods, such as a piece of bread or rice cake. To begin with she'll hold it in her fist, working hard to push the last mouthful in with the flat of her hand. In time, she'll learn how to hold food and other things between her thumb and forefinger. Never leave her alone with finger food in case she chokes.

Growing stronger

Your baby is growing stronger by the day and will be eager to flex her muscles and show off her skills. Some babies may even try to pull themselves up to a standing position from sitting by holding a parent's hands or piece of furniture. All of this is great practice for the next important milestones – learning to crawl, stand, and walk.

Social and emotional skills

Up until now your baby's main interests in life have been food, sleep, and you. Now her personality will begin to shine through.

Becoming sociable

You'll notice that your baby is becoming more sociable, turning to listen to voices around her. She'll also try and join in conversations, responding to your chat not just with baby babble but also with a range of gestures and facial expressions. Watch her look at herself in a mirror, too. She doesn't realize that she is looking at herself but she is interested in the baby she sees, and will gurgle away in the hope of a response.

Learning to sit

Thanks to all the wriggling, twisting, kicking, and stretching she has been practicing in her first six months, your baby can now sit up on her own – at least for a few minutes, and probably longer. Sitting up enables her to look around more easily, watch family members coming and going, and reach out for toys to keep herself entertained – if only for a little while.

SITTING UP
As a precaution, keep cushions around your baby to break her fall. At first she may use her arms for support, but she won't need them for long.

Loving you

Now that she can sit up on her own, your baby is much happier with her own company, but, as always, you are her favorite plaything. Has she dropped that toy again – and is she yelling for you to come and help? Maybe it's not the toy she's after, but a chance to smile and laugh with you.

The pleasure your baby takes in your company is a sign that she is forming a deep and genuine bond with you, her main caregiver. You may find toward the end of this month that if you vanish from sight for a moment, her bottom lip may begin to wobble as she fears you've gone forever. Return before the tears are in full flow, and she'll beam and bounce with happiness.

A sense of self

Part of this deepening attachment comes from her realization that she is a separate person from you. This is a huge and important milestone. Over the next few months, she may be increasingly anxious when separated from you. This can be upsetting, but it is perfectly normal and often continues through toddlerhood.

Meanwhile she will also start to develop attachments to other important people in her life – her siblings, grandma, or caregiver, for example. Gently encouraging these relationships will help her adapt to being without you when she needs to be cared for by someone else.

Activities to develop skills

There are several activities you can now enjoy playing with your baby to build up her physical coordination and social skills. Always remember to keep encouraging and praising her as she plays.

★ All babies love bubbles – and being able to pop them with their hands allows them to develop their hand–eye coordination as well as progress their understanding of cause and effect. Catch a bubble for your baby on the plastic wand and hold it right in front of her so she can reach out and pop it herself. Remember to clean her hands afterward so that she doesn't get soapy water in her eyes.

★ Encourage your baby's sense of fun by playing lots of bouncing games – hold her on your lap or on the bed and let her practice bouncing up and down, bearing as much weight as she can on her legs.

BOUNCING GAMES
Your baby will delight in the fun and movement of being swept up in the air and then bounced down again on your knees or a bed.

Language and intellectual skills

Your baby's everyday routines are now very familiar and she can also remember things that have happened before: she may start laughing even before you tickle her or say "Boo!"

Is it still there?

Your baby is also starting to learn about "object permanence." Up until now, when something disappears, your baby thinks it no longer exists. By the end of this month, she may be beginning to realize that just because she can't see something it doesn't mean it isn't there. You can see this in action by partially hiding a toy under a towel so that only part of it is showing. Chances are she'll try to lift the towel to find the toy – and in a month or so she'll look for it even when it's fully hidden.

Making conversation

By now your baby will be able to recognize her name and turn her head when she hears you calling. When she responds with her own babbles and gurgles, you'll begin to notice how much the tune and rhythm of her chatter sounds like real speech, and how she loves to repeat strings of familiar sounds such as "bababab" or "mamama."

Toy box

Pop-up toys
Pop-up toys will give your baby much fun. If you buy toys with pop-up animal characters, you can make appropriate animal noises and play guessing games with her.

Bubbles
Bottles of bubble mixture and a plastic wand are inexpensive and give great pleasure. Never let your baby grab hold of the wand or bottle.

Finger puppets
Use soft finger puppets with simply drawn faces that meet the right safety standards. Since your baby won't be able to hold them herself yet, they should also fit an adult's hands.

POP-UP TOYS
At this stage your baby will only be able to push the characters back down on the toy, but she will enjoy the satisfaction of making something disappear herself.

★ By now your baby will love to play with pop-up toys that burst out when a button is pushed or a dial turned. Let her push them back down herself, and she'll develop strength and coordination in her hands and arms.

★ Encourage you baby's social skills with a group of ready-made pretend friends – make finger puppets from cut-off gloves and give them eyes, ears, and a mouth – and show her how they can sing, dance, tickle, kiss, and chat to her.

Safety first!
Since most babies explore objects by putting them in their mouths, make sure all toys meet safety standards and that nothing can come off and choke a baby, especially any toys you make.

7 to 8 months

Your baby is very attached to you and is becoming demonstrably more affectionate. He is never happier and more secure than when you are together, and so he may become more clingy in unfamiliar surroundings or with people he doesn't recognize.

Physical development

Your baby may now roll from side to side with ease, flipping himself onto his back and over again. He may also sit for quite long periods and lean forward without falling over. However, he still can't twist sideways or swivel at the waist, and may often topple over when trying to reach for a toy. Comfort him if there are tears, but always let him try again.

Toward crawling

Although most babies learn how to crawl between eight and 10 months old, there will be some babies who don't begin to move until they are a few weeks older. To crawl properly, your baby needs to be strong enough to push himself up on all fours and then discover that by pushing down with his knees he can move forward. First crawls are often backward, and it may be a week or so before your baby learns how to move forward. Give him lots of praise whichever way he chooses to move around.

On his own feet

Pretty soon just sitting won't be exciting enough for your baby. Always looking for a new challenge, he will be eager to try standing, and may make his first attempt by, for example, hauling himself up in his crib while hanging onto the rails. To begin with he'll collapse in a heap or remain stranded and yell for help – he hasn't yet developed the balance or coordination to lower himself down gently. When you come to his rescue, take his weight and gently allow him to relax so that he can slide into a sitting position.

Social and emotional skills

Your baby is very affectionate – he'll kiss you when encouraged, hold his arms out to be lifted up, pet his toys. He'll love older children and will reach out toward them. But while he's sociable and outgoing one moment, he may be fearful and shy the next.

Meeting new people

When you meet people your baby doesn't know well, you may find he buries his head in your shoulders, clings to you, and cries. Becoming anxious if strangers directly approach him is one of his first emotional milestones. "Stranger anxiety" is normal, and can last for up to two years or so. Forcing your baby to be friendly or telling him he's being silly will undermine his confidence – instead, praise him when he does smile back. It is also worth encouraging newcomers to interact gently and slowly with your baby.

Separation anxiety

Around this age your baby may also become much more clingy and start crying when you leave him, even for a moment. This, too, is a normal stage of healthy emotional development. Reassure him with lots of physical affection and with time he'll learn that parents always come back!

Finger coordination

Your baby will now start to be able to pick up objects using his fingers and thumb, rather than just using the palm of his hand. His grip has developed, too, and it's now controlled and strong enough for him to be able to tear paper, for example. He'll also love banging anything he can get hold of, and enjoy the noise it makes. He will still want to put objects in his mouth, so be careful what you allow him to have within his reach.

DEXTROUS FINGERS
Let your child practice picking up a number of differently shaped objects.

Language and intellectual skills

Your baby can communicate well with gestures and facial expressions. His attention span is still short but it hasn't stopped his mission to explore everything he can put his hands on.

Gestures and expressions

You'll notice your baby's understanding of language is developing faster than his ability to talk. He is starting to respond to the names of familiar objects and people, glancing over at a favorite toy you've just mentioned, for example, or looking at his sister when you call her name.

Real speech is still some way off, but your baby has lots of ways of letting you know what he's thinking. Gestures, for example, are now a regular part of his repertoire – see him open and shut his hand if he wants something, shake his head or push you away if you're doing something he doesn't like, or try to wave when you say "Bye-bye." Watch his face, too – his facial expressions will convey a variety of emotions.

First words?

At this stage your baby recognizes his name and probably understands the meaning of a few other words and responds to them. And as he practices his babbling, his sing-song "conversations" may sound increasingly like real words, such as "dada" or "mama," so give him lots of encouragement and he will soon learn how to say them correctly.

Comparing sounds

The covering of a nerve that connects the ear to the brain – allowing your baby to pinpoint where a sound is coming from – is complete at about this age. Now he can compare his sounds with yours, and over the next few months he will increasingly attempt to imitate your sounds.

Discovery zone

As soon as your baby can propel himself in a chosen direction, he'll be into everything: cabinets, drawers, and wastepaper baskets. He has an overwhelming sense of curiosity to discover more about its shape, size, and texture. Does it taste good? Does it do anything exciting? Although he can use his hands to great effect, your baby will still put things in his mouth so take steps to child-proof your home (see pp.32–33).

I know you're there!

Your baby's understanding of objects is growing every day. He may now be beginning to see how things relate to each other – how a small box fits inside a big box, for example. More importantly, he's learning that something can still exist even if he can no longer see it. If you try the same experiment as last month (partially hiding a toy under a towel; see p.43), but this time completely cover the toy, he may now pick up the towel to find it.

Toy box

Plastic stacking cups
Try to buy differently sized cups in bright, contrasting colors that fit together well.

Squeaky, noisy, and musical toys
Babies love the sounds and noises of squeaky toys. They will also enjoy the repetition of hearing a particular little tune over and over again. Buy toys that they can grasp easily and operate themselves.

Nursery rhymes cassette

If your baby enjoys listening to you sing familiar tunes to him, record a few songs on tape, or play a cassette of nursery rhymes while he has a quiet time. Encourage other family members such as grandparents to record stories and songs also.

Activities to develop skills

Your baby is fast learning that he has a growing curiosity he needs to satisfy, and an urge to explore everything. Give him a selection of activities to keep him busy for a short while, or help him discover how to crawl toward the toys he is showing interest in.

★ Satisfy your baby's desire to discover new things by allocating him a kitchen drawer or cabinet that you have filled with safe but interesting household objects (*see below*). This will give him a chance to explore them in his own time, and will teach him more about the shape, size, and texture of different things. If he begins to tire of them, make a few small changes such as putting a ball in the bowl to rekindle his curiosity in it.

DOMESTIC DISCOVERY
Let your baby play with safe objects such as dish towels, plastic bowls and containers, measuring cups, a cake pan or colander, and plastic spoons.

Safety first!

Check that your baby's toys have approved safety standards, and never give him small objects that he can pop in his mouth and choke on. See also pp.32–33 for ways of ensuring a safe environment for him.

★ Help your baby learn more about the relationship between objects by giving him some plastic stacking cups in different colors, shapes, and sizes. It will be many months before he can fit them into each other the right way – or even stack them himself – but he'll enjoy trying. And when he needs a change you can build a tower and encourage him to try knocking it down – a game he'll love!

★ Singing his favorite rhymes together and giving your baby musical or noisy toys will help him practice his listening skills. Giving him age-appropriate toys that squeak when they are squeezed will help to develop his improving manipulation skills as well.

★ There are lots of ways you can encourage your baby to crawl: make sure he has plenty of opportunities by putting him down on the floor whenever you can; keep his knees well-covered so that crawling isn't painful or uncomfortable; and place a toy or something interesting just out of his reach to encourage him to try moving forward to grasp it.

BECOMING MOBILE
Place a favorite toy just beyond the reach of your baby and you'll soon find him using all of his ability to try to move along the floor to grab it.

8 to 9 months

Your baby's personality is really beginning to shine through, and as her physical skills continue to develop and she becomes more confident she'll start to show you that she really has a mind of her own when she wants something!

Physical development

Your baby may now be able to sit by herself for quite a while, as well as lean forward for a toy without toppling over. Don't expect her to play like this for too long, though: the physical effort of maintaining her balance is tiring, so after 10 minutes or so she'll be ready for a change.

Fast mover

Once your baby discovers how to move around – whether crawling or shuffling – she'll move faster very quickly. It'll be a question of "now you see her, now you don't," so keep a constant eye on her and check that there is no danger.

Hand control

As she now begins to spend less time putting things into her mouth and more time exploring them with her hands, her hand movements are becoming agile and controlled. You may notice, for example, that she turns the pages of her books herself, even though it's usually several at a time. And she can delicately guide small pieces of food accurately into her mouth with her fingers, making mealtimes slightly less messy than before. She can also bang two objects together by holding one in each hand, and watch her have fun with a plastic bowl and wooden spoon.

Standing tall

If she's managed it once, your baby will be eager to practice pulling herself to standing using either you or a nearby item of furniture for support. Initially she will cling tightly with both hands until she feels confident about putting all her weight on her feet, and may even stand on tiptoes. Don't worry, this is normal; with time she will put all her weight on her feet.

SAFETY CHECKS
Check that there are no unsteady pieces of furniture your baby might pull over as he moves. Too many accidents, and he may lose his confidence.

Pointing

Your baby may be starting to point, which is an important milestone. Controlling the index finger is the first step to mastering a pincer grip – being able to close the thumb and forefinger together to pick up tiny objects. It also helps her communicate with you as she may be able to point out things she wants. Encourage her by looking at books together and pointing at things as you name them. And let her practice picking up tiny things such as raisins or cooked kernels of corn.

Social and emotional skills

Your baby is quite a character now, with her own likes and dislikes. She may object if you take a toy away, or want to play the same game again.

Asserting her will

As her self-awareness develops, your baby will become more assertive and turn lots of everyday activities into a battle of wills! You may find she is beginning to arch her back when she doesn't want to be put in her car seat, or shake her head if you try to feed her something she doesn't like.

As frustrating as this behavior can be, don't forget how easily your little bundle of energy can be distracted! Her memory is short, and a fun toy or some fast thinking can refocus her attention: if she hates being dressed, sing her a funny song to help her forget why she made a fuss – or try redirecting your child's thoughts to what she can, rather than can't, do.

Shows of frustration

Your baby may become frustrated if she can't reach a toy she wants, for example. While it's hard not to rush in and hand the toy to her just to make her happy again, giving her extra time and encouragement may give her the motivation to figure out how to get it herself.

Good behavior

Your baby will now recognize the word "no" and associate it with an angry or unhappy look from you.

This doesn't mean she'll stop what she's doing, but now is the time for her to start learning – if she's heading into danger, for example, or hurting a friend or sibling. At this age her memory is still very short, so be prepared to say the same thing over and over again.

However, your baby loves to see you smile. Giving her lots of praise if she behaves well, or hugs and kisses for something positive, will encourage her to do things that please you, and also help nurture good behavior.

Language and intellectual skills

By describing and showing your baby everything you do, you can help her understanding of language.

Word recognition

By the end of this month your baby may be able to recognize up to 20 familiar words, such as "cup" or "teddy." She'll also laugh in the right places when you sing her favorite songs, look for her cup if you ask

Activities to develop skills

Around this age your baby can start to show off her problem-solving skills – as long as you can resist helping her when she faces a difficulty! Facing everyday challenges will help her figure things out for herself.

★ If your baby is becoming mobile, build a miniature mountain of cushions for her to help develop her crawling skills. Peep out from behind the cushions or use a toy to encourage her to climb over them. Her success will give her a real sense of satisfaction, help develop her sense of body strength, balance, and coordination, and prepare her for climbing real stairs.

Safety first!
Don't leave your baby alone since she may lose her balance and hurt herself. Never leave her alone in or around water.

OBSTACLE COURSE
Encouraging crawling babies to climb over cushions or even pillows is a fun and practical way of playing together. Stay at ground level so that you can encourage her.

★ Satisfy your baby's urge to explore, and her growing ability to problem-solve, with an activity board. Choose a board with cylinders that can whirl, dials that spin, and buttons that squeak. Show her how it works to begin with, and then let her have a go and investigate it in her own time. At first she may only be able to do the simple activities, like sticking her finger in a dial, but during the following months she'll soon figure out how to work the other activities.

★ Playing peekaboo and hide-and-seek with your baby at this age helps teach her about object permanence, and there are lots of variations: cover your head with a towel and let her pull it off, then let her try; hide behind the door with just a hand or toe showing, before popping out and gently surprising her.

her where it is, and associate actions with certain words, such as saying "Bye-bye" and waving your hand.

Her own babbling is developing all the time, and she may add new sounds to her vocabulary, such as "t" and "w." She may also try to imitate you coughing, for example.

Look what I can do!

She is also learning about cause and effect: every time she drops a toy from her high-chair you appear to pick it up again – a favorite game!

Toy box

Push-down toys

If your baby has a pop-up toy or a toy with buttons to push, encourage her to practice pushing down and releasing the buttons.

Household objects

When you are busy in the kitchen, your baby may love to play with some simple, safe kitchen utensils. Let her have fun with unused items such as a saucepan, plastic bowl, dish towel, and wooden spoon.

Toy piano

A toy piano or xylophone is a toy that your baby can grow into. For now, she will enjoy the random sounds she can make while developing her listening skills.

★ Fill a basin with water and, using different spoons, cups, and containers, show your baby how she can fill and pour. Emptying and filling games such as this are good for helping your baby practice her hand movements and develop dexterity and hand–eye coordination. Water games are great for bath time play, too.

★ Learning how to hear different sounds will help develop your baby's listening skills - and eventually progress her speech. If you play a familiar tune that she'll recognize on a xylophone, or a toy piano, it will spark her interest and may encourage her to try creating some wonderful sounds herself.

WATER GAMES
Playing with water is a great form of supervised entertainment. Always keep a gentle but firm hold on your baby as she plays near water.

CURIOUS NOISES
Don't worry if your baby's coordination skills have not developed enough to play this toy – this new curiosity is the start of listening to noises she makes herself.

9 to 10 months

Your baby may now be gaining immense pleasure from all his activities, as well as enjoying having lots of fun with you and other members of the family. His ability to understand language is growing in leaps and bounds and he's beginning to make a real effort to communicate with you.

Physical development

As your baby is now spending more time upright, playtime becomes more fun for him since he is able to see and handle his toys more easily.

Climbing stairs

If your baby is now an experienced crawler, he may be trying to attempt more challenging maneuvers such as crawling upstairs. While stair-climbing may help him learn how to judge height and depth and develop his sense of balance, for safety reasons it is important to install stair gates so he can't attempt them without you on hand to help. Going up is easier than coming down, and it will be a while before he's ready to learn the skills needed to make a safe descent.

Cruising

Very mobile babies may now be attempting a few steps while holding onto a piece of furniture. If your baby is becoming more confident, he'll soon discover how to move across a room using pieces of furniture as balancing aids. Learning how to "cruise" like this is the last physical skill your baby needs to master before he begins walking without assistance. If he reaches a favorite toy by maneuvering himself across the room like this, remember to give him lots of praise.

Attention span

Your baby's sense of his environment is growing rapidly. He now notices and is interested in people and things up to 10 feet (three meters) away. At the same time, his attention span is increasing: he is becoming more absorbed in activities he enjoys, and you'll find it harder to distract him when, for example, you need to take something away from him.

ABSORBED PLAYTIME
Your baby's concentration skills are improving all the time, enabling him to play with toys for a little longer.

Fingers and hands

By now your baby has mastered the pincer grip and is able to grasp things accurately between his thumb and forefinger. Self-feeding, for example, is now much easier, and his finely tuned hand–eye coordination enables him to pick up anything he comes across. This manual dexterity means he can now use toys as they were intended – putting blocks in and out of a box, for example. And he still loves dropping and picking up games – he drops, you pick up!

Visual skills

Since his birth, your baby has been refining his visual skills and now he can judge the size of an object up to three feet (one meter) away. He'll

know, for example, that a ball rolled from this distance will get larger as it comes toward him. Watch how he holds out his arms to catch it. Ask him to roll it back, and initially he may swing at it with no effect, but eventually he'll be able to return it in your direction.

Social and emotional development

Your baby is probably familiar now with his routines and really enjoys being included in family activities such as mealtimes. He's also becoming great company, and this month he may play his first jokes on you. However, expect him also to develop some new fears.

Activities to develop skills

Now that your baby is becoming more alert and aware of what is going on around him, introduce some indoor equipment such as a large plastic ball and an expanding tunnel. And help him improve his fine motor skills by giving him harmless objects to handle and explore.

★ Your baby may be starting to become aware of the noises animals make, so now is the time to introduce some animal songs into your repertoire. Look at animal books together and let him hear you mimic all the different sounds they make. Once your baby learns to imitate lots of animal noises, his success will encourage him to copy other sounds too.

★ If your baby loves moving objects from one container to another, why not make a surprise box full of interesting and harmless objects for him to handle, explore, put back in and take out again. To make the game more interesting you could wrap some items in paper – he'll love ripping them open to see what's hidden inside. Never leave your baby alone if you give him paper to play with since he may put it in his mouth and choke on it.

★ Satisfy your baby's need to explore with his hands – and encourage his sense of touch – with a "touch-and-feel" activity book that contains pictures and shapes made out of different textures.

TIME TOGETHER
A shared activity is valuable time for parents and babies to interact, and all the more enjoyable if parents can explain things and encourage their baby.

★ Babies at this age are intrigued by space – they love crawling behind sofas or around the back of chairs. Your baby will probably also love to crawl through a play tunnel. Roll a ball toward him inside the tunnel so that he can see how it works. As he becomes confident, he'll soon love being chased through the tunnel or hiding from you inside.

★ A daily trip out to the park or local playground is a good chance to spend time together. It also means you can encourage your baby's sense of spatial awareness, and improve his visual skills as you point things out to him.

EXPANDING TUNNEL
If you buy an expanding tunnel, check to see that any wire used in the frame is covered and sealed. These tunnels are often very lightweight and made of bright material.

His sense of humor

Your baby's first laughs were probably prompted by physical games such as being bounced on your knee or lifted high up in the air, and later by visual jokes such as you shaking your hair about or putting his bib on your head like a hat. Now he is more mobile, he'll enjoy teasing you by doing things you don't like – heading out through a forbidden door and then looking back to see if you're watching, or pushing the off button on the TV. He may also enjoy showing off to you by putting his plate on his head, for example.

Developing fears

At the other extreme, this is the time when your baby may develop fears about things that have never upset him before – the noise of a vacuum cleaner, perhaps. If he seems unduly scared of something, stay relaxed and comfort him and reassure him that he won't come to any harm. Slowly familiarizing your baby with the object of his fear can help conquer this tendency. For example, let him examine the vacuum cleaner once it has been switched off. Take things one step at a time and in time he will manage his fears.

Language and intellectual skills

By now your baby is beginning to communicate more and letting you know that he is an important family member with something to say.

Making conversation

Your baby loves interacting with people, and will enjoy social get-togethers such as mealtimes. He will try to join in conversations and may even initiate conversation. Now his strings of babble clearly follow the rise and fall of an adult conversation. And, although on the whole it still sounds like nonsense, it is important for you to listen and respond, since this encourages him to keep trying.

New sounds

Your baby may also be starting to use the beginning of words that sound as if they relate to specific things, such as "ca" for cat or "ba" for bath, for example. Complete words won't emerge for another few months, but trying to understand your baby's words – or invented words – and repeating what he might mean back to him will help him learn how to say these words properly over time. Seeing and hearing you trying to understand the sounds he makes will probably also give your baby immense pleasure.

Understanding language

Your baby's understanding of language is continuing to increase faster than his ability to use it to speak. In the meantime he may use gestures as well as sound to get your attention – perhaps waving at you or pulling at your clothes – and will even repeat himself if you don't understand what he is trying to say.

Toy box

Household objects

The simplest objects provide fun for a baby. He may like to pick up an orange from a small cardboard box and pop it back in again, or take dry clothes out of a plastic laundry basket and put his toys or a doll in it.

Touch-and-feel books

A selection of different activity books will give your baby a new perspective on the world. Choose strong, brightly illustrated books with clear images and interesting textures.

10 to 11 months

Your baby may be starting to behave more like a toddler if she is beginning to spend more of her time standing on her feet. And she feels more grown-up, too – she loves trying to do new things with you, and is a happy companion for you.

Physical development

At this age babies vary enormously in their physical achievement. Some are crawling; others have just started to sit, while some may be attempting to walk. Your baby will do things in her own time.

Leaning and twisting

Your baby's balance has improved tremendously. She can lean sideways while sitting without toppling over, and twist round to reach something behind her, enabling her to reach for things herself.

Standing alone

By now, early crawlers are likely to be spending a lot of time up on their feet and cruising confidently. Your baby may even attempt to take her hands away from her support and try standing alone for a few seconds. Be prepared for bumps and bruises, and give her reassurance if she falls. Her first solo step will happen soon and, meanwhile, she's working hard to perfect her balance and coordination.

Social and emotional skills

Your baby is keen to get involved in household chores, loves being with other babies, and may now become more attached to a comfort object.

Copying and helping

Your baby is understanding the world around her more clearly than ever before, and she wants to be involved in whatever is going on around her. If she sees you busy wiping her high chair after a meal or sweeping the floor, she'll want to join in and she may try to copy you brushing your hair or washing your face, too.

She may also try to help speed your progress when you dress her by slipping her arm into her sleeve, or getting her shoes for you to put on her feet. Make sure you always tell her what you're doing and why. Give her a chance to have a try too, although don't expect her always to get it right: many a baby has tried to brush their hair with a toothbrush, for example!

Making friends

By now, your baby will enjoy seeing other babies her own age – and may get excited when you invite friends around with babies of their own. She will happily play alongside another baby if they are put on the floor together, but don't expect too much interaction between them. For now, just sitting alongside another child is good for your baby. She can learn a lot just by watching them – and feeling at ease in company will help her take her first steps toward learning how to make friends.

Comforting objects

Around this time, lots of babies become attached to a special object such as a blanket or soft toy, which they insist on taking everywhere with them. Known as a "transitional object," this item will have a special place in your baby's life, helping her sleep when she's tired, and reassuring

Hand control

By now your baby has excellent hand control and can do lots of things for herself. For example, she can turn the pages of a board book one at a time, learn how to put blocks into shaped holes, or accurately roll a ball in your direction if you encourage her. And she can not only give you an object such as a block when you ask for it, but also release it at will into your hand.

THE ART OF LETTING GO
Mastering the art of letting go is an important step, since your baby can now place objects where she wants to.

her if she's unhappy, especially if you are not around to comfort her. This is especially true for babies still dealing with separation anxiety.

Your baby will probably rely on her comforter for some time to come. Only when she finds other ways to deal with upsets will she gradually give it up. Meanwhile, if you are concerned about cleanliness or losing it, try to have two identical comforters to hand in case one is mislaid or needs to be washed.

Language and intellectual skills

You and your baby may be able to communicate together well, and now that she is nearly a year old her understanding of what makes the world go around is developing fast.

Reacting to questions

Your baby may still not be saying very much, but her understanding of language and communication is growing in leaps and bounds. She can now follow simple questions such as, "Where is your cup?" and will probably reply by pointing or looking in the direction of the cup. If you ask a simple question such as, "Do you want a drink?" she may respond with a smile and move toward the cup.

If your baby has older brothers or sisters, they will find this a rewarding time, since they, too, can begin to interpret what she is trying to express.

Activities to develop skills

Now she is in her eleventh month, your baby is becoming more interested in how her toys move, fit together, or make noise. With her improved hand skills she can put objects where she chooses, so give her activities that will help improve these skills.

★ Now she can easily let go of objects when she wants to, your baby will probably enjoy playing with a simple shape sorter.

Start with your own version made out of a shoe box, with a round hole cut in the top and a ping-pong ball for putting into it.

If she enjoys playing that game, then you could try cutting a square hole in a box and this time giving her a block for inserting. This exercise will be harder than inserting the ball.

When she needs a new challenge, buy her a more complicated shape sorter to play with.

LETTING GO
Your baby's improved hand coordination will now enable her to place objects where she wants them. Putting plastic rings back on a ring post is a good exercise for her to try.

Understanding concepts

As your baby's intellectual skills develop you'll be able to watch her making more sense of her immediate world.

Now, when she sees a picture of a dog in her book, she'll perhaps relate it to her grandfather's dog or the dog she saw in the park, and begin to realize that, even though every dog she sees looks different, they are all in fact dogs. She can now also grasp the idea of opposites.

Toy box

Shape sorter

Shape sorters should be durable and incorporate a selection of simple, recognizable shapes. Make sure the shapes are not so small that they fit easily into your baby's mouth.

Board books

A selection of different activity books gives your baby a new perspective on the world. Choose strong, brightly illustrated books with clear images.

Toy telephone

Your baby will enjoy pretend toys such as telephones – especially those that make noises. Buy a safe, well-made version.

★ As your baby learns to turn the pages of a book, make sure she has plenty of them to look at, especially board books. Encourage some regular quiet time together so that books become part of her everyday life.

★ Establish her interest in the adult world with toys that mimic real objects, such as a toy telephone. Copying you is your baby's first step toward fantasy, or imaginative, play – and, by naming the objects she is playing with, you are helping her language skills too.

★ Show your baby how you can build a tower using blocks, books, plastic bowls, or even plastic cups. She may not be able to build a tower with objects yet, but being able to knock them all down herself will give her such a great sense of power – and a real understanding of cause and effect.

BOOKS FOR LIFE
Books are a valuable source of interest and learning for a child, even at this early age. You will both derive great pleasure from this activity if you make a point of doing it together.

With the help of your explanations, she will understand the difference between wet and dry, hot and cold, big and little, and in and out.

Linking objects to events

Your baby's understanding of cause and effect is now well developed – she knows exactly what will happen when she bangs her drum (it makes a noise) or drops her block (you will probably pick it up!).

She's also beginning to match objects to their intended purpose. For example, she'll put a toy telephone to her ear just as you do with a real telephone, or pick up the towel in the bathroom and wash her face with it. This is an important step forward, since she will use this understanding to help her when she starts to match what she says to the objects she wants to talk about.

11 to 12 months

As your precious baby approaches his first birthday, you will look back in amazement at the incredible changes that have taken place. He is now a little individual with a unique personality, a wide range of emotions, and a strong sense of his place in the family and his daily routines. He is bursting with life and energy, full of love and affection for those closest to him, and a real joy to be with.

Physical development

This month your baby may attempt to stand alone and even take his first steps unsupported. But don't forget that the speed of your baby's physical progress depends on his individual development and he should not be compared to other children.

First steps

Toward the end of this month your baby may take his first steps – a really exciting development. If he's perfected his balance while cruising around your furniture, he may start to let go occasionally, grabbing hold of something only if he totters. Once he reaches this stage, encourage him to walk toward you, or widen the gaps between the furniture.

Initially, he may manage only one or two steps before falling; encourage him to try again, and before long he'll manage more and more steps on his own. Moving the furniture slightly further apart will also help him gain confidence. But be prepared for your baby to go at his own pace - lots of babies don't walk until they are 13 or 14 months old, and some not before 18 months.

Self-feeding

Now your baby has much more control over his hand movements, he is more accurate in everything he does with them, including feeding himself with finger foods with no difficulty. Using a spoon isn't as easy to master, since it involves difficult hand–eye coordination in addition to good muscle control. But now he can rotate his hand he is much better at getting food into his mouth, although it will still be a messy business.

It is worth encouraging your baby to feed himself, since he may refuse to have someone else feeding him, and he shouldn't rely on you entirely for all his food. On the other hand, it's still too early to leave it all up to him. Although he may start each meal enthusiastically, he'll soon get distracted and you may have to intervene to ensure he eats enough.

Throwing

Exploring different objects is still one of your baby's favorite activities but now he will probably have stopped putting everything that he picks up into his mouth. How an object feels in his hands is now more important to him, and he will experiment more and more with his hands. For example, he will try to hold more than one item – such as two building blocks – in his hand at a time, although for a while he will drop one, and maybe both. And having discovered last month how to let go of something purposefully, he is now having great fun throwing things deliberately!

Social and emotional skills

As the person or people closest to him, you are still your baby's first love and the most important focus in his life, but at this age he also enjoys being with other people, especially other children and his siblings.

Your growing relationship

Your baby is very loving toward you and showers you with hugs and responds to kisses when he chooses to. He can also be self-focused, believing that he should come first when it comes to getting attention from you. At the same time, his sense of independence is increasing and his desire to explore means that he won't sit contentedly in your arms for long.

Mixing with other babies

Now is a good time to introduce him to other babies and children, particularly if he doesn't have sisters and brothers at home. He'll still want to stay close to you, but he will be fascinated to watch and imitate the other babies and toddlers around him. At this age, however, don't expect him to mix actively, join in, or share with the others. Your baby still thinks the world revolves around him and, while he'll be very happy playing alongside other children, he'll naturally assume that every toy is there just for him. He won't be able to understand the reasons for sharing for another year or more.

Copying good manners

Although at this age your baby doesn't understand how, or why, he needs to have good manners, he loves imitating you and his siblings. Learning the way you behave will help him get on with other people as he gets older. Even before he can talk, your baby can learn social rituals like how to wave bye-bye. And if he hears you using polite words, he is more likely to use those words himself once he can talk.

Language and intellectual skills

Your baby has been preparing for talking in lots of different ways, and his increased ability to concentrate will help him with his first words. His memory is also getting much better.

Preparing to talk

Most babies are still experimenting with sounds as they get ready to talk. By now they can use most vowels and many consonants. If your baby has stopped dribbling, this could be a sign that he's getting better at controlling his tongue, mouth, and lips. He may also be trying to imitate the last thing he heard you or someone else say. You may catch the odd recognizable word in among the gibberish!

First words

Some babies may be able to say two or three words by their first birthday, although usually only you and the rest of his family who are in tune with his routine may understand them. There may then be some weeks before your baby uses more words, which is quite normal.

Concentration and memory

You may notice your baby can listen to very short stories right through. This is partly because he can now understand you, and because he can give you all his attention for longer.

Your baby's developing memory and past experiences now affect a lot of his actions and behavior. You may notice this in the way he loves to cause chaos to his routine – for example, crawling away at top speed when you are trying to get him ready for a bath or put his coat on. Knowing what's going to happen next gives him a great opportunity to play a joke – at your expense!

Toy box

Pull toy

If your baby is becoming actively mobile, he will probably enjoy playing with a pull toy on wheels that he can trail behind him. These are often available in the form of animals or trains.

Soft toys

Soft toys can become treasured possessions. Choose dolls that have expressive or appealing faces to attract his attention to them.

Nursery rhymes

Nursery rhyme books and songs will give your baby huge pleasure and are excellent for helping his language development.

Activities to develop skills

Help your baby expand his understanding, and particularly his knowledge of the names of objects, with familiar songs and books. Try also to encourage him to share well-loved toys, and develop his coordination and rhythm by playing clapping games with him.

★ Your baby may now be able to hold his hands flat when he claps his hands together; if not, let him hold your hands as you clap them together. Let him sit on your lap, or on the floor facing you, so he can watch and join in clapping games and songs. Putting words, gestures, and music together will help with first words as well as giving him the chance to play with and imitate you.

CLAPPING GAMES
Action games will become more and more enjoyable for both of you as your baby anticipates the next step in a sequence or song.

SHARING POSSESSIONS
Although your baby is still too young to learn how to share properly, a simple game such as giving and taking will gradually reinforce the idea for him.

★ Play give and take with your baby by offering him something new to look at, then asking for it back when he's finished exploring it. If he gives it to you, praise him. If not, take it gently, thanking him and praising him.

★ Soft toys such as teddy bears and clowns and dolls will give him lots of play opportunities for many years to come. Use them now to help him learn social rituals – encourage him to kiss his favorites goodnight, or say goodbye when he goes out for the day.

★ Your baby will love listening to song tapes and looking at books again and again. This repetition will help encourage his first words and improve his memory.

★ If your baby is beginning to walk, he may be ready for his first push toy. At first you may need to help him along, but he'll soon enjoy pushing the toy himself.

Safety first!
Make sure that all soft toys and dolls have passed approved safety standards and do not have loose items such as buttons or beads.

Index

allergies, 21
assertiveness, 49
attention span, 53, 62

babbling, 15, 29, 30, 46, 55
beakers, 23
bedtime routines, 26–7
bonding, 42
books, 31, 55, 59

centile charts, 16–17
character traits, 10–11
chest infections, 19
chewing, 22
child care, 9
choking, 21, 23
comforters, 26, 57–8
concentration, 53, 62
conversations, 55
crawling, 15, 45, 47
cruising, 53, 61
crying, 27

dairy products, 21
developmental checks, 14–15
diarrhea, 19
drinks, 21, 23

earache, 19
eating, 20–3
emotional development, 39, 53–5, 57–8, 61–2
eyesight, 14, 53

fears, 55
fevers, 19
finger coordination, 39, 45, 49, 53
finger foods, 15, 22–3, 61
food, 20–3
food poisoning, 21
friends, 7, 57, 62
frustration, 50

games, 42–3, 47, 50–1, 54, 58–9, 63
genes, 12
gestures, 29, 46

hand control, 39, 41, 45, 49, 53, 57, 61
health checks, 14–15
hearing, 14, 29
hygiene, 33

illness, 17, 19
immunizations, 17
intellectual development, 39, 43, 46, 50–1, 55, 58–9, 62

language development, 15, 28–31, 39, 43, 46, 50–1, 55, 58, 62

manners, 62
massage, 34–6
memory, 62
milestones, 39

naps, 24–5
night feeds, 25

paracetamol, 17, 19
personality development, 10–13
physical development, 39, 41, 45, 49, 53, 57, 61

record keeping, 14, 16–17
rolling over, 15, 45

safety, 32–3, 43, 47, 50, 63
self-awareness, 11, 13, 49
self-feeding, 15, 22–3, 61
separation anxiety, 8–9, 27, 42, 45, 58
sitting up, 15, 41, 49
sleep, 24–7
snacks, 21
social development, 8–9, 39, 41, 45, 53–5, 57, 61–2
stairs, climbing, 53
standing up, 15, 45, 49
stranger anxiety, 8, 45

teething, 18–19
throwing objects, 61
toys, 26, 43, 46, 51, 55, 59, 62
twins, 12–13

walking, 53, 61
weaning to a cup, 23
word recognition, 50–1, 55

Acknowledgments

The author would like to thank Claire Legemah, Susannah Steel, Julia North, and Glenda Fisher for all their work.

Credits
Jacket photo: Jason Homa/Image Bank; **jacket design:** Nicola Powling
Indexer: Hilary Bird; **proof-reader:** Nikky Twyman
Models: Tali with Gil Krikler, Denise with Kymani and Kymarley Woodstock, Helen with Joseph Jack and Leo Stiles, Mulki with Wyse Ali, Janis and Maureen Lopatkin with Mia Lopatkin, Mr & Mrs Kiyomura with Eri, Michelle with Charlie Terras, Ivor with Ruby Baddiel, Rachel with Zoe Nayani, Maria with Jasmine Leitch; **hair and makeup:** Tracy Townsend

Consultants
Warren Hyer MRCP is Consultant Pediatrician at Northwick Park and St. Mark's Hospitals, Harrow, and Honorary Clinical Senior Lecturer, Imperial College of Science, Technology and Medicine.
Penny Tassoni is an education consultant, author and trainer. Penny lectures on a range of childhood studies courses and has written five books, including *Planning, Play and the Early Years*.

Picture Credits
Picture researcher: Cheryl Dubyk-Yates
Picture librarian: Hayley Smith

The publisher would like to thank the following for their kind permission to reproduce their photographs:
(abbreviation key: t=top, b=bottom, r=right, l=left, c=centre)

Bubbles Photo Library: Jennie Woodcock 24br. **Mother & Baby Picture Library:** Ruth Jenkinson 16bl. **Corbis Stock Market:** Steve Prezant 27tr. **Jacket photo:** Jason Homa/Image Bank

All other images © Dorling Kindersley. For further information see: www.dkimages.com